# The Art of Allowing

**HOW TO LET GO AND CONNECT TO THE DIVINE PLAN**

## Nicky Hamid

Humanity Rising Shortread Series

Volume 1

# The Art of Allowing

Copyright © 2023 by Nicky Hamid.

ISBN 9798392981472

All rights reserved. No part of this publication may be reproduced, stored in a retrieval system, distributed or transmitted in any form or by any means, including photocopying, recording, or other electronic or mechanical methods, without the prior written permission of the author.

Printed in the United States of America.

Author Contact

**https://remembersoultribe.wixsite.com/membership**

# Contents

1. INTRODUCTION ..................................................................... 1
2. CALLING IN YOUR TEAM ................................................... 3
3. TRUST YOUR OWN PROCESS ............................................. 5
4. CONSCIOUSLY LET GO INTO THE UNKNOWN ....... 7
5. BECOMING THE "WATCHER" OF YOUR OWN EXPERIENCE ........................................................................ 11
6. CULTIVATE YOUR INTERNAL SMILE ....................... 13
7. ON PRUDENT ACTION ..................................................... 14
8. PRESENCE OF MIND .......................................................... 16
9. BE PRESENT ......................................................................... 20
10. LISTEN TO YOUR BENIGN INNER VOICE ............. 22
11. SURRENDER TO THE LOVE THAT YOU ARE ....... 24
12. FLOWING IN OF GRACE ................................................ 27
13. LETTING GO LEADS TO BECOMING MORE ........ 29
14. LOVE EMBRACES WHAT IS .......................................... 31

| | |
|---|---|
| 15. LETTING OTHERS BE THEMSELVES | 33 |
| 16. BEYOND THE LOGIC OF THE MIND | 35 |
| 17. SEEING WITH THE EYES OF LOVE | 41 |
| 18. CALL IN MORE LIGHT | 43 |
| 19. MOVING FROM MIND TO HEART | 45 |
| ABOUT THE AUTHOR | 47 |

CHAPTER 1

# 1. Introduction

Get out of your own way.

You are a Divine Being at One in and One with the Source of All That Is.

Pure Essence of Soul that you are is about to fully enter into your Heart, and your body form, to merge and blend, to be a radiant Presence at Home in human expression. There is absolutely no way your mind can either comprehend or control any of it.

Who do you think you are?

What to do as the inevitable Shift in your Consciousness is unfolding?

Let us first remember that there is nothing that you need to know or to accomplish in any 'mindy' way. This mode of coping is done and over with.

Of course some prefer to use their mind, to extend and stretch it like exercising your body. And some are far more at home with feeling and intuiting their knowing. One way is not better than the other. It is more important to play and experiment.

It is not anymore about coming to a conclusion about anything. It is about exploring and discovering and sharing. It is not about agreeing or disagreeing with others. It is about being at home with your own journey and opening to other ways of seeing. It is about the joy in the light of your own discoveries and the discoveries of others rather than the acquisition of a discovery itself.

And for heaven's sake, don't take yourself so seriously. Apart from Lovingness, the single most important thing you can do is practice your 'ALLOW-manship'.

This small book presents you with little reminders about how to allow. Things we all know but are still opening up to as a continuous dynamic in our conscious Beingness, such that it becomes a flowing backdrop to all we do.

CHAPTER 2

# 2. Calling in Your Team

Allow the changes in you to take place. Do not try to rush it, you can't.

Pushing, contriving, worrying will just make it rough on you, and delay the inevitable, your choice to Be fully You. To be Present.

It does not matter if whatever is happening to you at the moment takes a day or several days or more. It is your time.

If any fear, any concern, any doubt arises, the Company of Heaven is on call. Ask for help and let go. They are here "in overtime mode" to be of assistance, for all you need is the contact of Love to be back on centre.

They are standing right next to you wherever you are. But You have to do it, it is your Divine 'opening' not theirs, you are "on the ground" not them.. And apart from this contact you already have all the wherewithal to flow through any circumstance. You are a Divine Being, becoming a Lighted Human in body. The illusion of separation is over and thus all suffering has and will dissolve.

Let it go.

Allow the Love to Flow.

**PS:** And if you are tired and sleepy, dizzy or disoriented, rest and sleep as often as you need and can. Don't push yourself. You are going through major rewiring, information downloads, and upping of your frequency band.

It is happening without your "doing" anything. Trust and care for the "body You" with the caress of this Divine You that you are opening to. It may not feel easy BUT it can be done through persistence, patience and with Ease and in Grace.

CHAPTER 3

# 3. Trust Your Own Process

If you know beyond all doubt that You are Divine then you will know that you are Love incarnate and that you are forever inseparable from All That Is.

Allowing then is based on three Trusts.

Trust in the benevolence design and function in all Creation. Trust in yourself in Essence, Presence, and Creative expression. And trust that everyone else is also that which you are.

And thus this day you can allow everything to unfold as it will. You already have all you need to action whatever emerges. The Universe will bring you anything you require for any moment. And if your moment requires you to relate to another they will have everything they need to lead them onwards as well. So there is no need to be concerned about anything. By being in your place whatever you do will be in perfect order both for you and all others who may be concerned.

So what are you thinking (and doing) when you try to preconceive or manipulate the future'?

CHAPTER 4

# 4. Consciously Let Go into the Unknown

What you have learned, through effort and struggle is what you cannot do and how society has defined you and what you are not.

In other words the illusionary non-self.

Making the Shift is about letting go to an energy that is totally taking care of you and everything.

This is a difficult one because you have always looked for someone to take care of you or for you to effortlessly take care of yourself. Now it is for you to have fun and choose happy, and allow the Divine that you are to do All the "heavy lifting", the working out, the timing, and creation of benevolent outcomes.

Surrender to Source and discover who you really are and what you are capable of. Shine On

PS: And how do you surrender to Source? To surrender is to "give up". to consciously 'give' what is in that moment (what you think you are) 'up' to an infinite knowing, the Divinity of You, that is all around and within you, but which is Unknown in that moment.

Giving up all mind interpretation of yourself or your story in any given moment by stopping, looking (watching), feeling, and listening to what is.

Giving up any trying, 'efforting', planning, or interpreting. Letting things be just as they are. When you go to sleep each night you are surrendering to Source.

Do it consciously.

Perhaps it was what Jesus was referring to when he said "I die daily". For when you sleep you are in the same place that you are when you are finished with your body. Surrender is to die to the little illusionary self and when we can do this consciously we will realise eternal wakefulness. And the energies now are with us to do just that right now.

Give up the struggle, it is all illusion. Hard or easy is simply a matter of choice moment to moment. If you look back and believe the memory of hard then so be it. But if you look now it is simply a matter of choice and it is so easy. And if you surrender then no matter how you feel you are "stuck" in your life circumstances, you will be lead to choice points that will miraculously release all the illusion.

Guaranteed, money back if not overjoyed by the experience.

## Art of Allowing

Yes, humans have preferred familiar and look for certainty of mind even when the unfamiliar may be less painful. The only way to break the familiar is to try the new. Try doing new things, things that break your patterns, things that you would like to do but feel a little scare with.

You will only find out what you are capable of if you walk into the fear. Fear is only lack of knowing. And facing your fears requires trust in yourself and trust in the Universe. You will only find your strength by taking the risks and trying. And there is no wrong choice nor can there be failure.

But to do this you have to be courageous enough to live and act without having to know exactly where it will lead to and what will follow. And your comfort with allowing can only come from your brave steps into the unknown. And the experience of finding out that the Universe is totally benevolent.

Dare to do things differently, think of new things, do the same things that you do through habit but do them differently (eg. use your eating fork with your non preferred hand).

Share your love more boldly, take small risks and always be grateful for the opportunity and for whatever results. Miracles will happen. Just you watch what happens when you dare to be yourself and try new things that you have always wanted to do but always put aside.

Allow yourself to be happy

CHAPTER 5

# 5. Becoming the "Watcher" of Your Own Experience

Awakening is not a denial of all that is human. It is coming back to meet it all with a fresh awareness because you are now not what you thought you were. You are an I AM awareness, a Divine Presence, that can love the whole journey and all the experiencing of it without becoming attached to any of it.

To be able to experience sadness and annoyance as well as love and joy without the need to put a story onto it and make a play and production about it. Allowing it to be felt and then to pass.

The same with thought, not to prop ideas up to be special and to be filed away and reinforced and strengthened by sorting more to solidify the original. But rather to enjoy and play with it, then let it go in an instant. Mind becomes an aspect of consciousness that is fluid and free. Thoughts are of the moment and in their spontaneity can be exciting, inspiring, insightful or profound, but we not always have to capture them as if the knowledge gained will be otherwise lost.

It is all about becoming the "Watcher" of your own experience.

Freedom becomes the freedom of being totally with and in your awareness and with the ever-present backdrop of your own Lovingness.

CHAPTER 6

# 6. Cultivate Your Internal Smile

If you are having trouble letting go, surrendering. Then the very next thing that happens to you, that you feel, or see, or experience, say "Yes" to it. ............"Thankyou". And smile within.

That is all. And instant by instant, in your remembering you will become everything you ever dreamed of and more, much, much more. It is the Law of your own unfolding. The Flow is here, then LOVE IS HERE, the Love IS your very Essence. The Universe complies and conspires and So It Is. Allow, and joyously follow just a tad behind. You will not believe how miraculous it all is. Your life is a conversation with the Universe, a conversation with God.

# 7. On Prudent Action

It is often so important to allow the other person to find things out for themselves.

In your zealousness, in your eagerness to let people see what you see, to know what you know, it is so easy to begin (perhaps unknowingly) taking the others energy. When we do so we are denying them an opportunity to take their own empowerment through coming to their own insights, their own truth knowing, in their own way. Knowing when to hold your tongue and when to speak, when to be still and when to act, requires 'prudence'. An almost forgotten word in the old reality. The way of balanced. Of when to speak and act, and when to be remain silent, and hold the space of love, the most fertile of grounds.

And there are no rules for this great virtue. Appropriate action is always in the moment and comes from Being in one's own Presence, letting your heart knowing direct, because love always knows when to support by touch and action and when the very best and most expansive support is to step back and watch. To be fully present in compassionate understanding requires this prudence. The knowing of prudence requires you to trust, observe and allow much, much, more.

Art of Allowing

CHAPTER 8

# 8. Presence of Mind

What do you need to do Now?

Simply pay attention.

Your experience comes from what you pay attention to. But you will never experience peace unless you can be THE OBSERVER. The I AM THAT I AM without even thinking that this is what you are. And you will REMEMBER.

Attention without intention. An unfocused attention because as soon as you focus your attention on anything, everything else is temporarily left out.

Haven't you noticed this? This is what we might call "Higher Mind". A Mind that contains the possibility of anything and everything. A state of mind that has not chosen and is simply Present.in the moment "empty of "mental mind thoughts

A Quantum Field Presence- The OBSERVER (Watcher).

It is in fact Presence. Presence of Mind. The You, that is not bound to anything special but allows All That Is as available as "no thing in particular".

So the idea of "mindfulness is turned on its head.

"Mindlessness" perhaps, the space between.......... "Divine Neutrality"

So I am suggesting you spend some time each day just being consciously Present, by choice, without focusing on anything. Doing nothing, simply watching, with a "soft", all inclusive awareness, with no attention on anything in particular just being Present without even the attempt of "trying" to be Present, for that is not possible.

This is your STRONG point where all is solved and dissolved. Through practice you will become aware of a kind of "undoing", a softening of boundaries between ideas, things, and a gradual inclusiveness, of everything that presents itself to you as your world of experience.

As you cultivate this Observation from "higher ground", Soul being that you ARE in fact, the clarity and purity of Mind begins to emerge. Thought with a cutting edge. And thus, when you do choose to pay attention to anything, you begin to see it in greater clarity, purity, simplicity and connectedness to everything else.

Your stories drop away, and the extent to which you get drawn and distracted gets weaker.

**PS:** You see it is like you got stuck in "lower mind" (thinking). Let me call it "particle mind" And you took on an agreement to perceive your reality as constructed from particles just like frozen moments that are strung together in a time sequence. In order to do this you had to pay attention to these particles as if they stood for something permanent when they are not.

So now you are learning not to pay attention to them any more than a passing moment, so as to allow much, much, more to be available to you.

You get to Create from your deep, Soul Call Preferences. A more unfocussed attention allows you to begin to be in, and comprehend, Flow. The Waves of the "out there" which is in fact the knowing of the "in here". And this growing quality of Mind can only be Present when you let go of the need for, or fixed truth of, particular choice as constructed through "little mind". And for all this to unfold it occurs in a field of your Divine Lovingness. This is why it appears as HeartMind.

I am simply "pointing to" your expansion in your own way. And whatever I have said is not it. Your Truth is in a depth of your Feeling and cannot be captured through logical mind.

As soon as you attach a special and fixed meaning to anything it disconnects, it separates one experience from another. It is all in Feeling you know.

And thus, you cannot love anyone unless you Love everyone. And it has to start with Yourself for that is the Inner and the Inner reflects and projects outwards for expansion to be possible.

# 9. Be Present

Being Awake.

How do you know that the modality you are practicing is going to work, the teacher you are listening to is going to lead you further into your truth, the job you are moving to is going to be more fulfilling, etc?

When you are Present, or what you are doing makes it easier for you to be Present, anything can work.

Practice this modality or that, use this crystal or that, listen to this person or someone else, work as a shop assistant or a healer, meditate or simply walk in a garden, dream or create, .......... it all works when you can be fully Present within yourself.

Love Is and You Are.

Joy and Happiness accompany The Presence, Your Holy Presence, and It WORKS everywhere.

You are not just in the Flow.

You ARE FLOW.

Thus wherever you are, whatever you are doing..........SHOW UP.

CHAPTER 10

# 10. Listen to Your Benign Inner Voice

All the knowing, all the knowledge we will ever need will come to us as we need it. It is Present always within the expanded Auric Field of Soul you ARE. It is already there (in your Luminous Field as light 'packet weave' of countless layers of light frequency.

It is like our Soul Being is the secret agent "Director" saying "I will make it available to you (personality Human Self) on a need to know basis". It is a fail safe from the confusion and mind numbing detail. The dealing with the miasma of thoughts we are bombarded with , from our internal dialogue, and the constant scrambled frequencies beaming to us from the disintegrating "matrix movie" that we have been born into.

If only we would stop and Listen to that benign inner voice of Freedom and Love.

So much more simple and uncluttered, don't you think?

How much do you really Trust yourself, mighty Soul? And how much can you Trust the Universe, Source, God?

How willing are you to act without having to know exactly how it will turn up and turn out?

Absolutely everything and anything is available through a Love filled command.

**PS:** You do not have to see the changes in this Now for them to be happening. If you are shifting then know everything just IS.

Step back, get quiet, observe, choose, and then act. The old operating system was react, regret, and then blame (mostly yourself).

Look quietly, deeply within, naked and honestly, and see the beauty of your own reflection.

# 11. Surrender to the Love that You Are

Love is the key.

Love is the Allowance of the Grace and the energy of ONE.

Love is the movement of the Divine Mother through you and the stillness of the Father anchored in you.

It is the interconnectedness and the state of Divine Union.

Love is the being of that state of Home with Self.

It has descended and you have been penetrated more than you can imagine at this time (the Presence of your Divine Presence)

Recognizing that You are the essence of One, waking up is not about you rejoining. it is about you allowing and remembering the truth and the wholeness of who you have always been from moment to moment.

You have always carried the essence of Love.

The quantum leap is simply you, breaking away from the story of "Am I loved, am I lovable?" to the full acceptance that you are Love and that everything and everyone carries the same Essence.

The only thing you are leaving behind is a Drama, a story that was created by Humanity in its 'darkest' hour, to control and prevent you from remembering.

It is OVER now. We are not getting or running away from anything. We are stepping into what is real and what has always been.

This life you are having is entirely different to any other incarnation because you are allowing the truth of your abilities to Shine through.

Gaia can now restore her full glory without the impact of the cruel drama. And as these things are streaming away from your body, your frequency is heightening, and you are starting to feel lighter, giddy and sometimes extremely fatigued.

Lie down and surrender to the Love that you are. And just because, in your life at present, you can only put energy in for small spurts, does not mean that nothing is being done.

Haven't you felt the growing stillness within and the dissolving of the old fears. It is this stillness where so much is being accomplished. In fact, much, much more than you ever accomplished working hard all day.

This is the new way the way of $5^{th}$ dimensional beingness. Less is more because in your Lovingness and the simplicity of Being, there is the knowing and there is a miraculous effortless economy of doing and of creating.

And inexorably you return (the Sacred Self that you are is "coming back") from this stillness this great and enfolding Love.

CHAPTER 12

# 12. Flowing in of Grace

There is no more fight. There is nothing more to battle. That is all old stuff and it is all over. All your thoughts are but a passing panorama of our human experience.

The only thing you have to win over are your own thought patterns.

This is accomplished by a gentle, loving understanding, and a non-judgmental attitude to self.

All the beliefs you have ever held are up for comprehending, review, and transformation.

It is through the total allowance of the Great Flow to enter you. In this Flow, Grace begins to enter, emerge in and through you. It becomes eternally present in your awareness. In this Grace you are flooded with a Presence that begins to take your breath away. You breathe more deeply, more consciously and it flows in and through your life, touching everything about you and around you.

The knowing of this leads you to let go more, because in your life, you begin to see that absolutely everything is taken care of. It all happens so easily, so effortlessly.

There is nothing more to fix, to release, to "work" through. Just a simple choice of experiencing the up and down motion of human experience as an opportunity to test your wings and discover what thoughts you will permit to remain, or you will allow to pass without any attention.

You find that you can create by the simplest intention of thought and that you no longer wait for results because you know, without any shadow of doubt, that in the Flow, in this state of Grace, all is most beautifully present even though you do not see it at the time.

Life becomes a magnificent dance of allowance in Love.

Thus, in fact, is there no more battle, no more win or lose. There are brief moments of appearing to hold on and then there is Flow.

Allow Grace to enter. Let go.

CHAPTER 13

# 13. Letting Go Leads to Becoming More

Knowing that life will give you something better than whatever it asks you to give up.

This is the secret of being fearless, of being at peace with yourself. When you realize that life is one, beautiful whole movement, a FLOW. And it cannot contradict itself. That life is not in conflict with anything it does within itself. And that we, as human beings, have the foundation of that very stuff within our Soul.

We only resist things simply because we think that life has come to take something away. And in a way it has, but it brings to us always something more. Something that tells us that what we were is but as seed to a great flowering. Life comes along to disturb us into new possibilities through our recognition of a higher purpose. You are in a vortex of your own discovery, and as the spin, your spin, takes you on around and around, and if you allow, you never come back to the same place for the vortex you are in takes you "up and up", deeper and deeper "within and without".

You first learn to ignore your doubts and step back from them. Then seeing the doubts pop up, smiling, and saying "No thank you". Then seeing them float by becoming fewer and fewer and hardly consequential at all. Eventually they will only impinge if you happen to focus deliberately.

Drop ever so gently into the FLOW.

Let go……Let go……Let go.

CHAPTER 14

# 14. Love Embraces What Is

If you are grumpy then that is the part of you that you are experiencing, if you are happy then that is part of you, if you are sad then that is OK too.. It is all quite perfect and is not to be dismissed but just felt as part of who you are.

If a feeling arises that seems a part of something in the past then, instead of holding to the story that initiated it, just see it, and come directly back to what you are feeling and allow it to be as an experience now without a story or interpretation of "right' or wrong", "good" or "bad".

Love is an embrace, a total allowance of what IS. And you are now to love yourself totally just as you are.

Everything arises in you to be seen and felt from the eyes and heart of Love. To be seen with the strength of your Will and Knowing of yourself.

There is nothing to dissolve or resolve. You cannot get rid of anything, you can only allow it to be present, to know, and in the Loving who you are, in your entirety, it weaves all your experience into a most beautiful signature that IS YOU.

Who said you had to be perfect or that it was possible?

Allow yourself to be current with who you have become through everything you have "been". Everything, but everything that has happened to you has been positioning you to be where you are now. And all the people, places, and opportunities you need are available to you right now for your most perfected journey.

The Universe can only say "YES" to you. Can you say "YES" to you, whatever you are /experiencing?

Shine On

CHAPTER 15

# 15. Letting Others Be Themselves

Allow others to be as they choose to be.

Let's be honest, this is exactly what you have chosen for you and you will be satisfied with nothing less.

You do not have to like what they are choosing but you must be able to allow that they also are Divine and on a human journey of their own Soul choosing.

There is no way you will see things exactly as they do. Each of us is a unique facet of Source, reflecting Creation and choosing experience that contribute to the complete Diamond LIGHT.

You do not have to keep butting in on their life and trying to change them and especially their perception of you. So what, that they do not appreciate or want to even hear your view of reality. Let them be.

## Art of Allowing

Knowing why only perpetuates the illusionary web that maintains separation, since how can you really know the nature and expression of another's journey.

Mind your own business. …… Ouch!!

And in allowing them to be, you free yourself to be who you are with no proviso for others having to change first.

In your allowing, you allow yourself to choose how you will behave and interact with anyone, and it will be based on the Truth of You and the expression you choose, in any given moment, based on your relationship to your own Lovingness and willingness to connect in that moment.

There is no more subtle, and not so subtle, trying to manipulate others to see how you see.

So dear reader, allow others to be.

You do not have to be near them, or want to be near them, in order to unconditionally Love them for who they are.

Shine On

# 16. Beyond the Logic of the Mind

You will never Know until you are able to curb the extreme tendency to want to understand everything with your mental mind. Mind is much more extensive and encompassing than mere thought.

You are a multidimensional being and as you are being inextricably drawn to your fuller state of Being you will just have to let go of the thought processes you have used in the past.

Thus the memory lapses, the confusion as soon as you take the "out there" of human affairs and try to manage them. The head spinning and headaches, strange, uninterpretable dreams, and all the thoughts arising that have to be nullified, etc, etc.

You have to go out of your mind, to come to your senses in Mastery.

You just cannot do it the old way.

Logic will not work anymore.

HeartMind (5D), your own Lovingness has to be chosen first. To realize and Know that you know far more than thoughts can tell or speak of. Knowledge through deep feeling tone is your Now way of knowing.

Thoughts arise from feelings, not the other way round. You have to feel something before a valid thought can arise.

You are just going to have to let go and trust if you want to know more.

And no one can give it to you. They can only point the way.

You will just have to trust yourself and your own subtle feelings.

The more you Love what you are, the greater the Trust. And the greater the Trust and watching and listening within, the more fluid and expansive and embracing is your Knowing.

"Little" mind will just have to take a back seat and wait for each new view of the horizon in front of you to reveal itself.

**PS:** What resonates is your "higher" heart knowing, which has nothing to do with logic or words. This is why your Living, Loving, Shining Presence is the only convincing demonstration of the reality of WE.

So if you still seem to be dealing with old issues that you thought you had cleared, you have not failed, you are still well and truly on track.

As a fully conscious being, you are becoming totally familiar with all the nuances of mind and emotion and you are to become a Master of your Mind. You have done your time being "lost" in 3D.

Stop SEEKING. You have arrived on the Ascension "platform". Everything is arising, step by step by Divine Design, the Law of Your Own Unfolding. You simply need to TURN UP, BE PRESENT and openhearted.

And all the Old Stuff is coming up. Why? BECAUSE IT IS LEAVING.
This includes everything that you see "out there" in the human "movie", which is locked into a system that has no energy that supports it any longer.

You are transforming DENSITY through your body. Watch and LET GO.

If you "lock" yourself into your own Fearless, Loving, Freewill Beingness, you do so for the whole Human Collective. You lock yourself into the Benevolent Conditions underlying All Change you see going on "out there". You automatically align yourself to the New World Earth Dream such that whatever is emerging from the Shadows of human experience is turned "upside down" (reverse) even if you cannot see how. Look beneath the shadow elements, Divine Light of our intentions is working Its "magic" and "miracles". Be steadfast in your Faith and Trust of God Force.

You have the power to create from any thought. Thus, you are creating your world through the thoughts and feelings you own.

Thoughts from your longing and desire of what to create (move towards) and avoid (move away from).

When someone has hurts you, you are rerunning the thoughts that created the hurt feeling in the first place.

Choose your heart then 'Watch" the thoughts and emotions, they are just thought/feeling with bodily sensations and you can change them anytime you choose.

Previously you may have taken all the Stuff "out there" personally, but you just cannot do this anymore if you want to drop the pain.

The great gift is that, if you allow even the smallest reaction it hurts so much because its lack of resonance with your Truth, reverberates through every cell in your body now.

Let it leave with hardly any attention. Do it in the moments that they arise in. Stop looking for them. Since there is only now, and that is the only place you can be, you can only create in that moment.

Hurt is feeling unloved. Turn it around, always turn it around. Instead of "they hurt me" feel where the feeling is and then say "I hurt me". "I hurt me when I said............" you told yourself an unkind lie about you and then you believed it.

Remember, everyone does things or says words that are hurtful because they are hurting.

And these lies have mostly occurred through other's thoughts that came when you were a child and were given little support to develop your own beliefs. It was thought that directed it, and since you did not want to take your own power (for whatever reason) you projected your own feelings onto the world and into beliefs about what others thought about you which made you feel powerless to do anything about your own feelings.

But it is just thought. It is your thought with an emotion attached to it and you will feel hurt until you stop playing the powerless game. The game that your thoughts are not your own. That is all over now. You are waking up.

Take no thought too seriously, before it has been seen from your heart. Choose the thoughts you wish to have and then let them be, let them come easily. And they will, as you are more compassionate with yourself, and see yourself constantly through the eyes of Your Love

Be not too attached to any for they will all change as you expand your consciousness.

Shine on.

CHAPTER 17

# 17. Seeing with the Eyes of Love

Everyone has a story.

I have a sad one and a happy and even comical one, full of the gifts of my experience.

And it all depends whether I am telling it from heart or head knowing, from joy or judgment. And this is always a choice.

A choice between the person I thought I was a little while back when asleep, or the person who I know I AM now I am awake and Remembering.

Living is all about Heart. Finding the Love within, seeing with the eyes of Love.

That seeing is what connects and unifies us all.

The world and all its creatures become more amazingly profound.

## Art of Allowing

The Love you experience everywhere reflects the Love you are, as you are experiencing it.

And then others around you begin to change (or they fade out of your Now experience).

You are inviting "versions" of them that match your Lovingness. It is felt and known, known and felt, simply by you being who you really want to be and others will be touched by who you ARE. It will call to them who they ARE

And as you learn to Love Fearlessly you see it reflected back at you day by day.
It is happening NOW, can you feel it?

Inhale well and feel deeply, sacredly.

Take nothing too seriously.

Take everything through your Heart but take nothing "to heart".

You are magnificently HUman.

CHAPTER 18

# 18. Call in More Light

Don't be impatient Precious Souls.

Everything is in a beautifully orchestrated Divine timing. There IS a Great Plan of the unfolding of HUman Consciousness. No one, no sentient Being in Form or Spirit knows the exact "moments" and manner it will pan out. That is up to us All.

Each of us is adding to this momentum of transformation to Beautiful HUman just by calling in more and more Light and Becoming the Love that you are.

Many of Us have been Present here (incarnate) with a Knowing of the general drift of what would be presented to us all, for a long time. It is now coming to fruition step by step.

When you find yourself swirling in confusion and immersed in emotions or thoughts that are unsettling your balance, Stop. Pause. Take a breath, hand on heart. Become a witness to all that you are feeling.

Take another deep breath.

Move your awareness from your mind and gently centre it in your heart.

You are currently experiencing a moment of potential growth. If we want to live in peace and harmony, then we have to find our centre, the source of our own life within.

As you feel into the energy that is moving through to your heart, you already know what to do about whatever is in front of you next in your life.

There is simply an intelligent action emerging from deep within you.

Your choice is whether or not to allow this action to move naturally from the invisible realm of your Soul Essence into the visible manifestation of your circumstance.

Will you allow this growth this Flow to occur?

# 19. Moving from Mind to Heart

The mental mind can only guess what the heart knows. Your "little mind", the mental mind, you have fashioned in the fires of duality and separation, judgment and self-blame.

In the Flow of Now it has only a whisper of place. All its 'knowing' is based on supposition and second guessing. It has no accurate say before the experiencing of anything. Only by dropping all sense of its predominance and importance, will self be freed unto Self. Let it go. Allow the fog to clear of its own accord.

No, there is nothing wrong with you experiencing, the mind haze, in the not being able to get your thoughts straight, nor your words fluent, or in your memory "losses", or increasing periods of "no mind". It is all part of the shift in consciousness you are making.

Be as the stillness, the quietest lake, the softest breeze, and you will be Present with yourself in Truth, in the here and now.

You will be Home, you will be in the Knowing of HeartMind. A higher Knowing beyond thought.

The Mind that knows always the Truth from the Eternal Now. With the clearing comes the exquisite clarity for freedom and focus, for choice in any given moment of Present And thus WE say...... "Allow all thoughts to drop into your heart". Then you will KNOW.

There will be no doubt.

Shine On.

# About the Author

Nicky was born just outside London with bombs raining from the skies during the WWII Blitz.

He was born into a large family, with both parents working class who were well read, aware, and very liberal freedom thinkers. Immigrated, at 9 years old, he grew up in New Zealand.

He has seldom lost sight of his childhood Innocence and Knowing of his connection to "Spirit" realms. He has walked with the Ascended Masters throughout his early life.

Dyslexic, especially with reading and writing, Nicky overcame such difficulties to gain a Masters and Ph D. in Psychology. He taught at Universities, especially in Self Awareness, Human Potential, and Social and Spiritual Psychology for 40 years while maintaining a spiritual mentoring Practice with clients around the world.

Nicky conducted awareness workshops and spiritual retreats in NZ, Australia, UK, USA, India and China.

Dubbed by his University Colleagues and students as "Professor of Happiness".

He has posted his own writings, twice a day on Facebook, for 14 years now.

Written several books – available on Amazon.

**Latest Books:**

First two volumes in the Ascension Reminder Series. Humanity Rising: A Journey from Fear and Control to Love and Freedom. Volume 1. (Sept. 2021).

Beautiful Human: A Lion Heart and Angel's Touch. Volume 2. (Feb. 2023).

**New Humanity Rising Shortread Series**

The Art of Allowing: How to Let Go and Connect to the Divine Plan. Volume 1. (Oct 2023)

Finding Peace of Mind: How to Break Free of Emotional Thought Loops. Volume 2. (Oct. 2023)

New Ways of Being: Making Significant Shifts in Your Consciousness. Volume 3. (Oct. 2023)

## CONTACT POINTS WITH NICKY'S WORK:

**Website:**

https://remembersoultribe.wixsite.com/membership

**Website: For Private Mentoring Sessions**

https://remembersoultribe.wixsite.com/membership/private-session

**Facebook**:

https://www.facebook.com/nicky.hamid.5/V

Please visit and join a thriving Soul Tribe

Printed in Great Britain
by Amazon